Fire Trucks

by Mary Lindeen

FIRE DEPT.

2057

E-10 SNC

BELLWETHER MEDIA • MINNEAPOLIS, MN

Note to Librarians, Teachers, and Parents:

Blastoff! Readers are carefully developed by literacy experts and combine standards-based content with developmentally appropriate text.

Level 1 provides the most support through repetition of high-frequency words, light text, predictable sentence patterns, and strong visual support.

Level 2 offers early readers a bit more challenge through varied simple sentences, increased text load, and less repetition of high-frequency words.

Level 3 advances early-fluent readers toward fluency through increased text and concept load, less reliance on visuals, longer sentences, and more literary language.

Whichever book is right for your reader, Blastoff! Readers are the perfect books to build confidence and encourage a love of reading that will last a lifetime!

This edition first published in 2007 by Bellwether Media.

No part of this publication may be reproduced in whole or in part without written permission of the publisher. For information regarding permission, write to Bellwether Media Inc., Attention: Permissions Department, Post Office Box 1C, Minnetonka, MN 55345-9998.

Library of Congress Cataloging-in-Publication Data
Lindeen, Mary.
  Fire trucks / by Mary Lindeen.
    p. cm. — (Blastoff! Readers) (Mighty machines)
Summary: "Simple text and supportive full-color photographs introduce young readers to fire trucks. Intended for kindergarten through third grade"—Provided by publisher.
  Includes bibliographical references and index.
  ISBN-13: 978-1-60014-059-4 (hardcover : alk. paper)
  ISBN-10: 1-60014-059-9 (hardcover : alk. paper)
  1. Fire engines—Juvenile literature. I. Title.

TH9372.L56 2007
629.225–dc22   2006035261

Contents

Fire trucks
speed to
a fire.

Fire trucks have loud **sirens** and flashing lights.

Firefighters drive
fire trucks.
Firefighters
fight fires and
help people
in trouble.

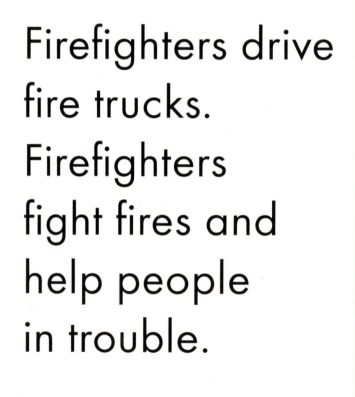

Many fire trucks
carry water.
Water can
put out fires.

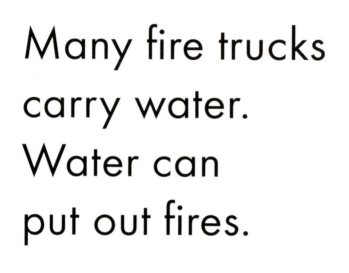

Fire trucks carry **hoses**. Firefighters use hoses to spray water on fires.

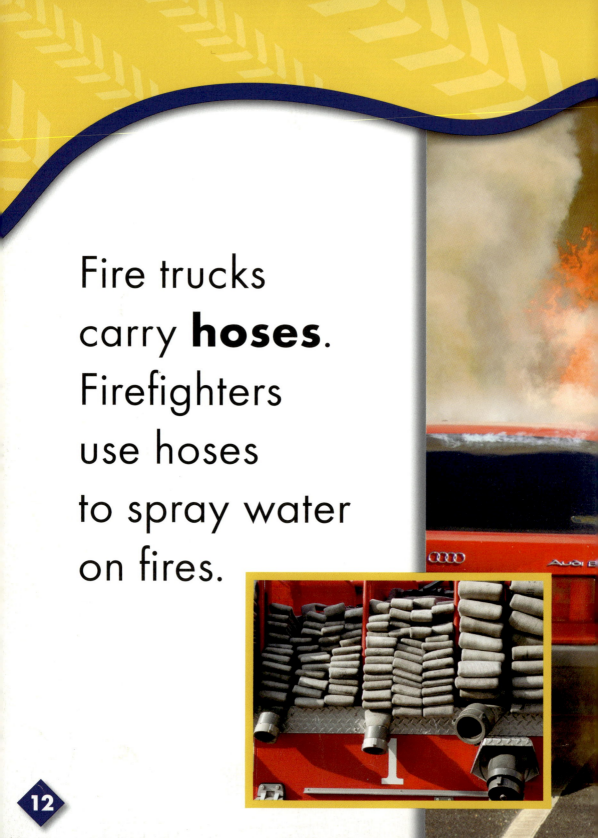

hose

Fire trucks
carry **tools**.
A firefighter
uses an **axe**
to break into
a burning house.

axe

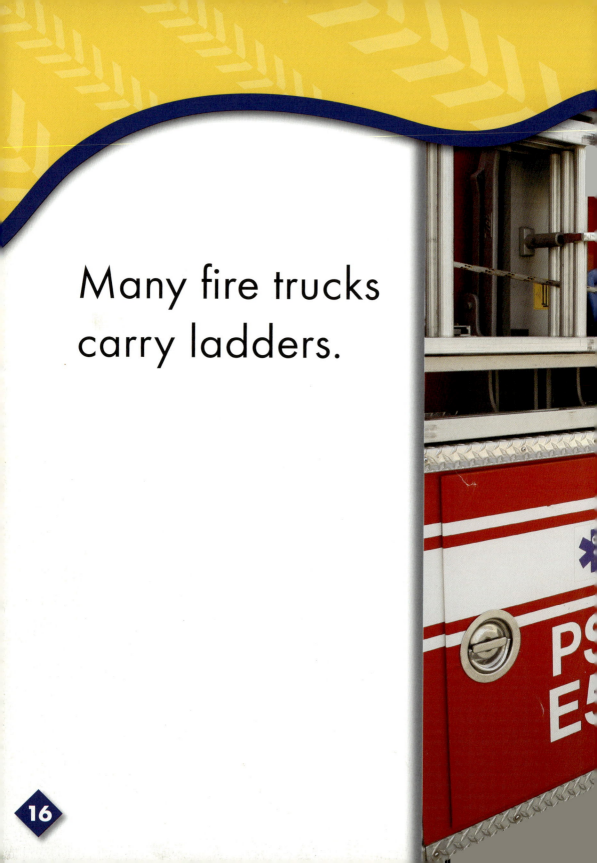

Many fire trucks carry ladders.

ladder

Ladders can
reach fires
in high places.

The fire is out.
The fire truck
returns to the
station.
It is ready for
the next fire.

Glossary

axe—a sharp, heavy object with a long handle that is used for chopping

hoses—long rubber tubes; water flows through a hose and squirts out the end onto the fire.

sirens—horns that make a loud, sharp sound; fire trucks use sirens to warn cars when they are passing.

tools—objects used to do a job

To Learn More

AT THE LIBRARY

Gordon, Sharon. *What's Inside a Fire Truck?* Pelham, NY: Benchmark, 2003.

Hoppey, Tim and Eida De La Vega. *Tito, The Firefighter/Tito, el Bombero*. Green Bay, Wisc.: Raven Tree Press, 2004.

Roberts, Cynthia. *Fire Trucks*. Chanhassen, Minn.: Child's World, 2007.

ON THE WEB

Learning more about mighty machines is as easy as 1, 2, 3.

1. Go to www.factsurfer.com

2. Enter "mighty machines" into search box.

3. Click the "Surf" button and you will see a list of related web sites.

With factsurfer.com, finding more information is just a click away.

Index

The photographs in this book are reproduced through the courtesy of: GSK, front cover; blphoto/Alamy, p. 5; Stuart Elflett, p. 7; ML Harris/Getty Images, p. 9; SuperStock/age fotostock, p. 11; JJJ, p. 12; EML, p. 13; Michal Strzelecki, p. 14; Mark Coffey, p. 15; Stephen Coburn, p. 17; Micah May, p. 19; Rocky Reston, p. 21